D1065108

Braces
for Cori

Written by Christine Florie
Illustrated by Christine Tripp

Children's Press®
A Division of Scholastic Inc.
New York • Toronto • London • Auckland • Sydney
Mexico City • New Delhi • Hong Kong
Danbury, Connecticut

For Paige and Corinne, my greatest inspiration
—C.F.

For my grandsons Brandon, Kobe, and Reece
—C.T.

Consultant
Eileen Robinson
Reading Specialist

Library of Congress Cataloging-in-Publication Data

Florie, Christine, 1964-
Braces for Cori / written by Christine Florie ; illustrated by Christine Tripp.
p. cm. — (A Rookie reader)
Summary: Cori is apprehensive about getting braces, but once she has them she decides they are not that bad.
ISBN 0-516-25136-8 (lib. bdg.) 0-516-25286-0 (pbk.)
[1. Orthodontics—Fiction.] I. Tripp, Christine, ill. II. Title. III. Series.
PZ7.F6646Br 2004
[E]—dc22

2004009326

1 2 3 4 5 6 7 8 9 10 R 14 13 12 11 10 09 08 07 06 05

Cori liked her teeth,
but she needed braces.

Her teeth were not very crooked,
but they were not very straight.

5

6

Why couldn't her teeth stay as they were? Cori began to worry.

What if her braces stuck
out like T.V. antennas?

What if they looked like
train tracks?

"Don't worry Cori," said Dr. Green. "I will make your teeth as good as new."

11

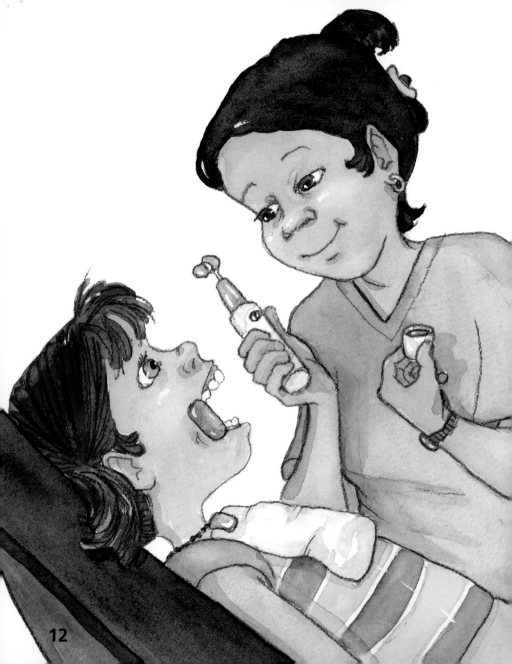

First, Dr. Green brushed
Cori's teeth.

Next, she glued the braces on.

Then, Cori picked a color.

Dr. Green gave Cori a mirror
so she could see her new braces.

Cori was surprised.
Her teeth looked the same.
The braces were blue and gray.

"It will take time for your teeth to straighten, Cori," said Dr. Green.

At school, Cori's friends wanted to see her new braces.

25

The lady at the bank liked how they were blue.

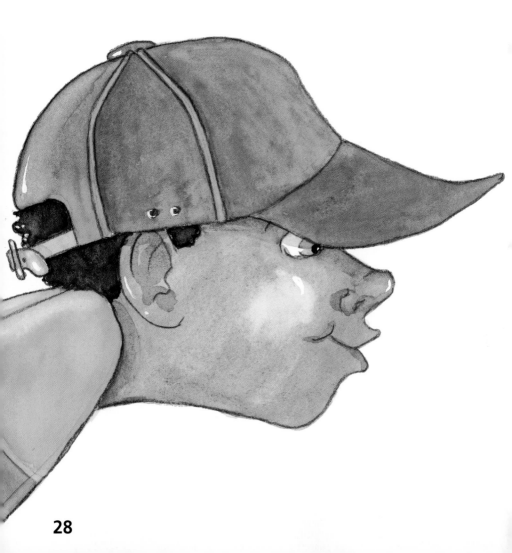

Her softball team thought they
were cool!

"Maybe this won't be so bad after all."

Word List (86 words)

a	Cori's	it	see	time
after	could	lady	she	to
all	couldn't	like	so	tracks
and	crooked	liked	softball	train
antennas	don't	looked	stay	very
as	Dr.	make	straight	wanted
at	first	maybe	straighten	was
bad	for	mirror	stuck	were
bank	friends	needed	surprised	what
be	gave	new	T.V.	why
began	glued	next	take	will
blue	good	not	team	won't
braces	gray	on	teeth	worry
brushed	Green	out	the	your
but	her	picked	then	
color	how	said	they	
cool	I	same	this	
Cori	if	school	thought	

About the Author

Christine Florie is a children's book editor and writer. She lives in Mahopac, New York, with her husband, two daughters, and a black Labrador retriever. When not editing, writing, and visiting the orthodontist, she enjoys cooking for her family, reading, and spending time with friends. She has also written *Lara Ladybug* in the *A Rookie Reader®* series.

About the Illustrator

Christine Tripp lives in Ottawa, Canada, with her husband Don; her four grown children Elizabeth, Erin, Emily, and Eric; grandsons Brandon, Kobe, and Reece; two cats; and one very large, scruffy dog named Jake.